D0463028

ALL ABOUT WINTER

People in Winter

by Martha E. H. Rustad
Consulting Editor: Gail Saunders-Smith, PhD

Mankato, Minnesota

Pebble Plus is published by Capstone Press,
151 Good Counsel Drive, P.O. Box 669, Mankato, Minnesota 56002.
www.capstonepress.com

Printed in the United States of America, North Mankato, Minnesota.

012010
005654R

Library of Congress Cataloging-in-Publication Data
Rustad, Martha E. H. (Martha Elizabeth Hillman), 1975–
People in winter / by Martha E. H. Rustad.
p. cm. — (Pebble plus. All about winter)
Summary: "Simple text and photographs present people in winter" — Provided by publisher.
Includes bibliographical references and index.
ISBN-13: 978-1-4296-2201-1 (hardcover)
ISBN-10: 1-4296-2201-6 (hardcover)
1. Winter — Juvenile literature. I. Title. II. Series.
QB637.8.R87 2009
508.2 — dc22 2008003335

Editorial Credits
Sarah L. Schuette, editor; Veronica Bianchini, designer; Marcy Morin, photo shoot scheduler

Photo Credits
Capstone Press/Karon Dubke, all

Note to Parents and Teachers

The All about Winter set supports national science standards related to changes during the seasons. This book describes and illustrates people in winter. The images support early readers in understanding the text. The repetition of words and phrases helps early readers learn new words. This book also introduces early readers to subject-specific vocabulary words, which are defined in the Glossary section. Early readers may need assistance to read some words and to use the Table of Contents, Glossary, Read More, Internet Sites, and Index sections of the book.

Table of Contents

It's Winter!

Winter is here.

It is cold and snowy.

Winter days are short.

What We Do

Teresa and Julian wear coats, hats, and mittens when they go outside.

We play in the snow.
The wet snow makes
good snowballs.

We play winter sports.
Lilly and Jim go skiing.

Winter Celebrations

We celebrate winter holidays.
Anna gives her grandma
a gift on Christmas Eve.

Carter plays
with a dreidel
during Hanukkah.

Harrison reads
about the seven days
of Kwanzaa.

Jane's family stays up
until midnight
on New Year's Eve.

Winter Fun

We have fun
outside in winter.
What do you
like to do in winter?

Glossary

celebrate — to do something fun on a special occasion or to mark a major event

Christmas — the holiday that celebrates the birth of Jesus Christ

dreidel — a toy with four sides that spins like a top

Hanukkah — a Jewish festival that is celebrated in December

holiday — a festival or time of celebration; people usually take time off work, school, or regular activities during holidays.

Kwanzaa — an African-American holiday that is celebrated for seven days in December

Read More

Rustad, Martha E. H. *Today Is Snowy.* How's the Weather? Mankato, Minn.: Capstone Press, 2006.

Schuette, Sarah L. *Let's Look at Winter.* Investigate the Seasons. Mankato, Minn.: Capstone Press, 2007.

Internet Sites

FactHound offers a safe, fun way to find Internet sites related to this book. All of the sites on FactHound have been researched by our staff.

Here's how:

1. Visit *www.facthound.com*
2. Choose your grade level.
3. Type in this book ID **1429622016** for age-appropriate sites. You may also browse subjects by clicking on letters, or by clicking on pictures and words.
4. Click on the **Fetch It** button.

FactHound will fetch the best sites for you!

Index

Word Count: 96
Grade: 1
Early-Intervention Level: 12